THE ADVENTURE BEGINS

DUNGEONS & DRAGONS

D&D

WELCOME TO THE MULTIVERSE OF D&D

Immerse yourself in the stickerology of the world's greatest roleplaying game.

DUNGEONS & DRAGONS®

DUNGEONS & DRAGONS®

NOTABLE HEROES

◇

These figures of legend play a compelling role in the lore and story lines of D&D.

GUENHWYVAR

A friend of Drizzt, this black panther lives on the Astral Plane and is summoned through the magical powers of an onyx figurine.

TASHA

The Mother of Witches, Tasha adventured across the world of Greyhawk and became the ally and enemy of many famous adventurers, including Mordenkainen.

MINSC & BOO

Fabled heroes known throughout the Sword Coast, Minsc and his hamster companion, Boo, have "kicked butt for goodness" over the years, defeating monsters while saving lives.

DRIZZT DO'URDEN

This drow elf defied an evil goddess and her cult, fleeing the Underdark for freedom aboveground. Now he and his companions defend the surface world from any— rogue wizards, tyrants, even gods—who would harm it.

MORDENKAINEN

A peacekeeping force and agent of true neutrality, Mordenkainen has created some of the most powerful spells throughout the realms.

These terrifying antagonists play a compelling role in the lore and story lines of D&D.

TIAMAT

With five heads, each representing a different color of chromatic dragon with corresponding abilities, the massive dragon god Tiamat aims to consolidate her powers and rule the Realms.

VECNA

Seldom is the name of Vecna spoken except in a hushed voice. Vecna was, in his time, one of the mightiest of all wizards who forged a great empire through dark magic and conquest. In the end, he became a feared lich.

THE TARRASQUE

A fifty-foot-tall dinosaur-like monster that can swallow just about anything in a single bite, the fear-inducing tarrasque has a huge appetite that's driven him to snack on an entire town within minutes.

DEMOGORGON

Demogorgon's psychic disruption field generates frenzy and fear in the minds of those nearby. He is traditionally portrayed as titanically large, leaving a swath of destruction wherever he passes.

XANATHAR

Arguably the most powerful and well-known beholder of all, Xanathar runs a massive criminal network of rogues called the Xanathar Guild.

COUNT STRAHD VON ZAROVICH

A Darklord from the nightmare realm of Ravenloft, this powerful villain is an ancient vampire who rules over the village of Barovia.

ACERERAK

A terrifying lich and one of the most powerful wizards in existence, Acererak created his own torture dungeon called the Tomb of Annihilation to funnel souls into his phylactery.

ICONIC MONSTERS

The most recognizable monsters, these core stars are in the DNA of D&D.

SPECTATOR

A lesser type of beholder, spectators are foul and deadly aberrations.

OWLBEAR

It is possible to tame an owlbear, despite their ferocity, to serve as a trusted pet or mount.

MIND FLAYER

Mind flayers, or illithids, are psychic tyrants who use their telepathic abilities to subjugate and control entire civilizations.

BEHOLDER

Covered with one large eye and ten eye stalks, armed with teeth, and protected by multiple forms of magic, this beholder lies ready to attack from its lair.

DEATH TYRANT

Watch out for undead beholders called death tyrants, which still retain some of their magical abilities.

GNOLL

Gnolls are feral hyena-like humanoids who prowl the borderlands, devouring the flesh of their slaughtered victims.

DISPLACER BEAST

These catlike beasts love to hunt and do it even for sport, but they are difficult to fight due to their unsettling ability to appear to be several feet away from their actual locations.

Chromatic dragons believe all the treasure in the world belongs to them and that their destiny is to rule the world.

GREEN DRAGON

Belligerent green dragons live in dark forests and exhale great clouds of toxic gas.

RED DRAGON

Proud red dragons live in mountain caves and deep underground. They scorch their prey with their fiery breath.

WHITE DRAGON

Ferocious white dragons dwell in arctic ice caves. Their breath can freeze their foes in solid ice.

BLUE DRAGON

Vain blue dragons burrow beneath desert sands and blast their foes with bolts of lightning.

BLACK DRAGON

Cunning black dragons dwell in dismal swamps and spew blasts of acid to dissolve their prey.

THE METALLIC DRAGONS

Metallic dragons amass treasures and relics that relate to their personal history and memories, or to protect the world from dangerous magic. At some point in their lives, they gain the ability to assume the forms of humanoids and beasts.

BRASS DRAGON

Talkative brass dragons live in deserts. Their breath can either burn with fire or put their foes to sleep.

GOLD DRAGON

Wise gold dragons live in secluded stone retreats. They breathe fire or a gas that weakens their foes.

COPPER DRAGON

Mischievous copper dragons live in dry, rocky caves and can spew acid or a gas that slows their enemies.

SILVER DRAGON

Noble silver dragons make their lairs on remote mountain peaks. Their breath freezes or paralyzes their foes.

BRONZE DRAGON

Inquisitive bronze dragons live in sea caves. They exhale lightning or a gas that drives their foes away.

GOLD DRAGON

Their distinctive rippling flight motion arguably makes gold dragons the most elegant in the air.

The multiverse brims with peril and many of the dangers are monsters. Here are a few you might encounter throughout your campaign.

CHIMERA

Treasure-hoarding and stubborn, these territorial monsters can be flattered with the right gifts.

MANTICORE

These territorial flying pack hunters fire tail-spike projectiles.

TROLL

Trolls eat anything they can catch and regrow lost limbs with unnatural speed. They fear only fire.

KOBOLD

These dragon-worshipping toadies keep their own tiny treasure hoards hidden in their networks of small tunnels and clever traps.

PURPLE WORM

These gargantuan burrowers are attracted to loud noises and consume everything in their path.

TROGLODYTE

Watch out for these warlike underground dwellers that have a persistent stench and an unending hunger.

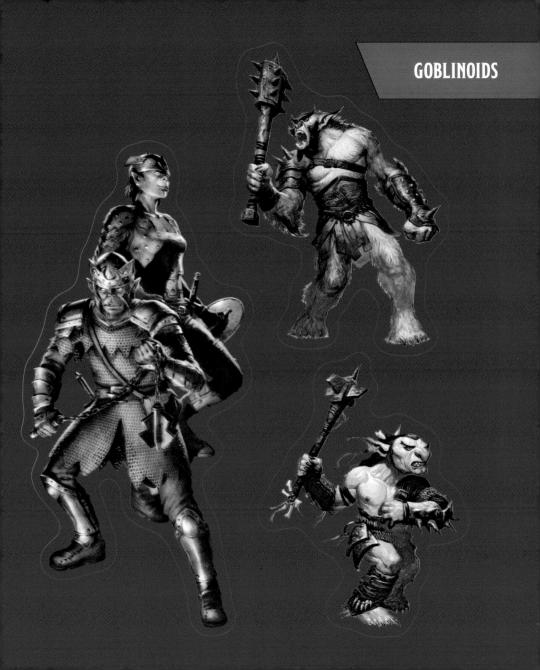

GOBLINOIDS

The three related species of goblins, hobgoblins, and bugbears can be formidable bullies.

BUGBEAR

Bugbears are often surprisingly stealthy bruisers with a love of carnage.

HOBGOBLIN

Hobgoblins have expertise with some military strategy and mastery of beasts.

GOBLIN

Goblins, the smallest of the bunch, are tenacious and extremely dangerous in large numbers.

RUST MONSTER

Medium-sized and subterranean, these monsters corrode ferrous metals and eat the resulting rust.

After a dungeon's creators depart, anyone or anything might move in. Intelligent monsters, mindless dungeon scavengers, predators, and prey alike can be drawn to the darkness of a dungeon.

MIMIC

Shapeshifting predators, mimics are able to disguise themselves as inanimate objects to lure their prey.

HOOK HORROR

Omnivorous pack hunters, hook horrors communicate by clacking their hooks loudly against nearby surfaces.

GRAY OOZE

These piles of liquid stone slither and strike like snakes.

GELATINOUS CUBE

Step out of the way of these transparent blocks of ooze that absorb and consume all living tissue.

BLACK PUDDING

Mounds of heavy sludge, black pudding will dissolve everything they consume.

UMBER HULK

Be careful: these mind-scrambling monstrosities burrow into underground walls and spring out as their prey passes.

HAUNTS & HORRORS

Face your fears! Terror stalks the realms as undead creatures lurk in the shadows of the night.

DEATH KNIGHT

Death knights are paladins who die after a fall from grace, without seeking atonement.

DRACOLICH

They are a cross between a dragon and a lich.

DEMILICH

Extra dangerous, demiliches have boiled it all down to just their skull with no body required.

LICH

You can't defeat these undead wizards without destroying their well-hidden phylactery—the special talisman that contains their soul.

ZOMBIE BEHOLDER

These mindless corpses are dead beholders that have been reanimated through necromantic magic.

GIANTS

CLOUD GIANTS

are creative, clever, and proud, and are evenly divided between good and evil. They live on cloud-covered mountain peaks or in castles in the clouds.

STORM GIANTS

are amicable, despite their association with thunder and lightning. They live in cloud castles, mountain peaks, or underwater.

Giants are members of an ancient empire whose remnants dot the lands they once ruled. They often belong to a caste structure, the ordning, which determines their status through a combination of their skills and qualities.

STORM GIANTS

can get up to 28 feet tall.

STORM GIANT ARMOR

FIRE GIANTS

are ruthless and militaristic, and dwell in hot places such as volcanic regions or hot springs.

FIRE GIANT

STORM GIANT

GIANTS

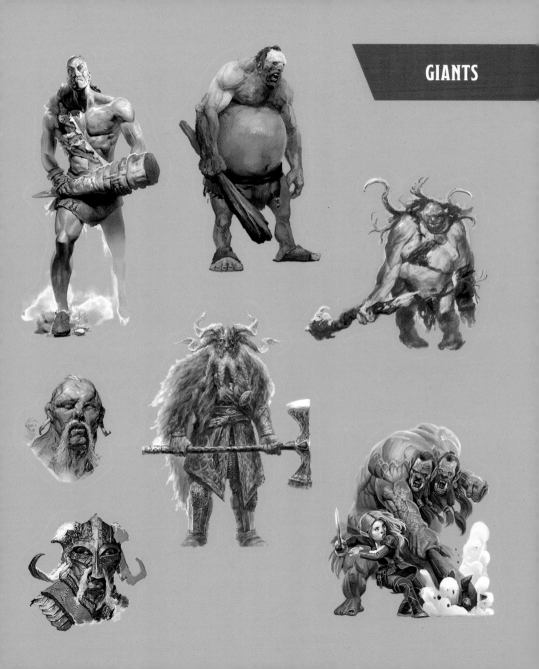

GIANTS

HILL GIANT

STONE GIANTS can be found in deep caves and are mostly playful and artistic.

HILL GIANTS derive their name from their habitat. Most are wanderers who rarely think beyond their immediate desires.

FROST GIANTS are marauders who plunder their territory for resources. Each warrior crafts a signature piece of armor from the remains of their fallen foes.

FROST GIANT

ETTIN are stinky two-headed giants and double the trouble.

FROST GIANT

HUMANS

Humans believe themselves to be the most adaptable and ambitious people among the common peoples. (Other folk may disagree . . .) They live fully in the present—making them well suited to the adventuring life—but also plan for the future, striving to leave a meaningful legacy.

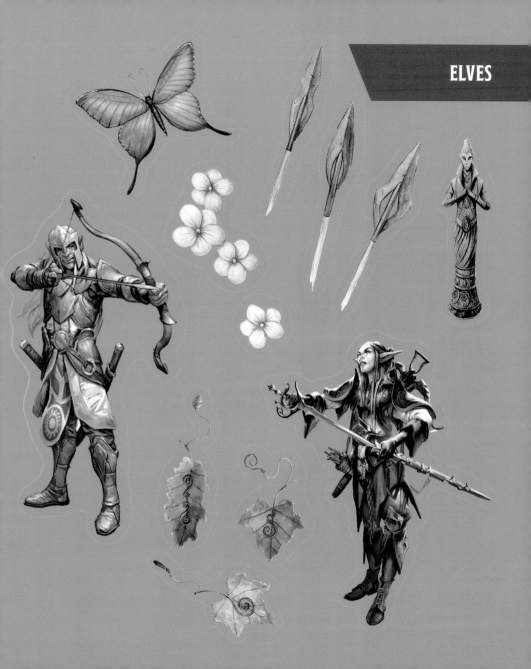

ELVES

Whether wood, high, or drow, elves often prefer endeavors that let them travel freely and set their own pace. They also enjoy leveling up their martial and magical prowess, and adventuring allows them to do so.

DWARVES

Bold and hardy, dwarves are often known as skilled warriors, miners, and workers of stone and metal. Although they feel a deep connection to clan and home, dwarves might venture out into the world seeking treasure, the approval of a god, vengeance for their kin, or an ancestor's lost relic.

DWARVES

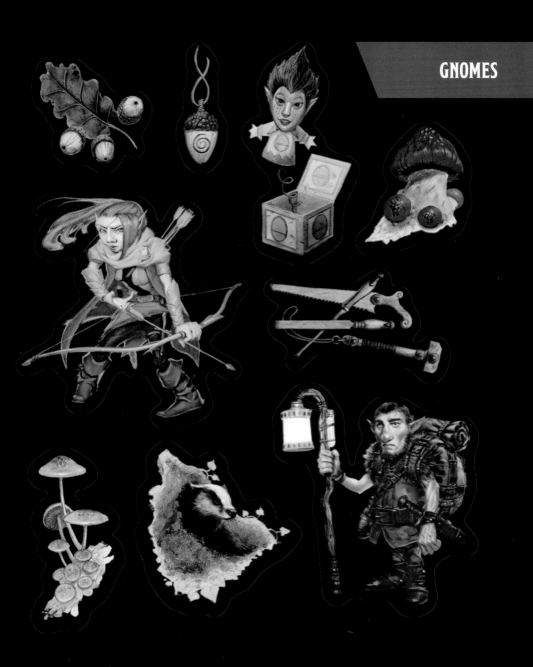

GNOMES

Gnomes' boundless
energy and enthusiasm
for living shines through
every inch of their tiny
bodies. They squeeze every
ounce of enjoyment out
of their 300 to 500 years.
Many gnomes are skilled
engineers, alchemists,
tinkers, and inventors who
aren't afraid of failing and
laughing at their mistakes.

DRAGONBORN

Descended from dragons, dragonborn walk proudly through a world that often conflates them with their fearsome heritage. They value skill and excellence in all endeavors and hate to fail.

DRAGONBORN

TIEFLINGS

Originally created by a literal deal with a devil, tieflings appear as a combination of the mortal and the infernal. Lacking a true homeland, tieflings know that they have to make their own way in the world and that they have to be strong to survive. Though their trust and loyalty are hard-won, a tiefling can be a ride-or-die friend for life.

ORCS

Orcs can be found living in traditional nomadic communities, urban centers, and everywhere in between. Not all orcs are warriors, but those who train as fighters are legendary for their endurance and strength. Like humans, their morality is individual and differs from orc to orc.

FIGHTERS

Fighters know there's a weapon to solve any problem. Slogging through waves of bad guys and coming home with treasure that amplifies their martial ability is extremely satisfying work for this combative core class.

HUMAN FIGHTER

TIEFLING FIGHTER

GNOME FIGHTER

DWARF WIZARD

Wizards live and die by their spells. They learn new spells as they experiment and grow in experience. What sets a wizard apart from other magic users is that their power comes from the study of magic.

HUMAN WIZARD

TIEFLING WIZARD

GNOME WIZARD

WIZARDS

CLERICS

Divine agents with the power of gods—and a sturdy mace—on their side, clerics channel the helpful magic of healing to assist allies and sling powerful spells that harm and hinder foes.

DWARF CLERIC

DWARF CLERIC

HUMAN CLERIC

ROGUES

HUMAN ROGUE

You won't know a rogue is stalking you until it's too late. Rogues rely on skill, stealth, and their foes' vulnerabilities to get the upper hand in any situation.

DROW ELF ROGUE

BARDS

Adventurous singers,
performers, and storytellers
whose acts are literally
spellbinding, bards weave
magic through stories and
music to inspire allies,
demoralize foes, manipulate
minds, create illusions, and
cause distractions.

ELF BARD

HUMAN
BARD

**ELF
DRUID**

Animal-loving,
shapeshifting nature
enthusiasts, druids cast
spells inspired by and
oriented toward nature and
animals—the power of tooth
and claw, of sun and moon,
of fire and storm.

**GNOME
DRUID**

**HUMAN
DRUID**

**TIEFLING
DRUID**

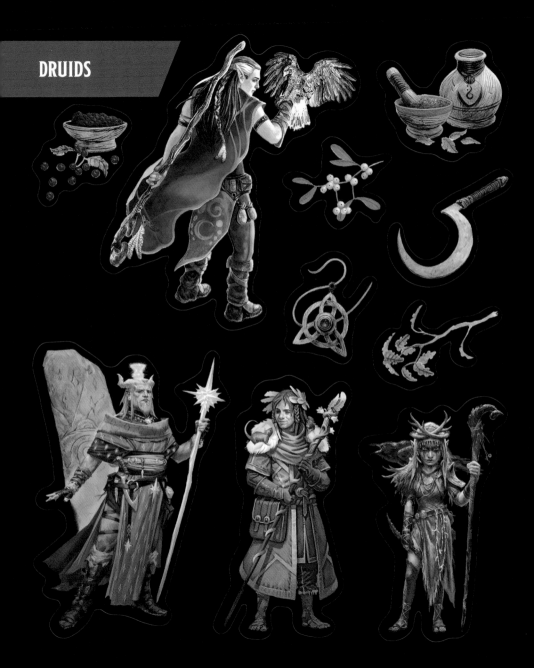

DRUIDS

BARBARIANS

Here's their secret: they're exactly who you think they are. For every barbarian, rage is a power that fuels not just a battle frenzy but also uncanny reflexes, resilience, and feats of strength. They embrace their animal nature—keen instincts, primal physicality, and ferocious rage.

HUMAN BARBARIAN

HUMAN BARBARIANS

Armor-clad champions righteously beating back the forces of darkness, all paladins are united by their oath to stand against the forces of evil.

**AASIMAR
PALADIN**

**ORC
PALADIN**

PALADINS

RANGERS

Watchers in the wilderness and guardians of the borderlands, rangers have a calling to defend the outskirts of civilization from the ravages of monsters and humanoid hordes that press in from the wild. They learn to track their quarry as predators do, sometimes bolstered by an animal companion.

ELF RANGER

HUMAN RANGER

TIEFLING
SORCERER

Magic is in the blood of
sorcerers, and it likely takes
some effort to keep it at
bay. Some wield magic that
springs from an ancient
bloodline; others stumble
into it through cosmic
chance.

TIEFLING
SORCERER

HUMAN
SORCERER

ELF
SORCERER

SORCERERS

WARLOCKS

Seekers of the knowledge that lies hidden in the fabric of the universe, warlocks are defined by pacts they've made with otherworldly beings that help them unlock magical effects both subtle and spectacular.

HUMAN WARLOCK

ELF WARLOCK

HUMAN WARLOCK

TIEFLING WARLOCK

MONKS

Monks study a magical energy that most monastic traditions call ki, an energy that flows through living bodies. Using ki, monks channel uncanny speed, strength, and elemental power into their unarmed strikes, and some eventually gain mastery over the bodies of their foes.

WAY OF MERCY MONK

DROW ELF MONK

DRAGONBORN MONK OF THE ASTRAL SELF

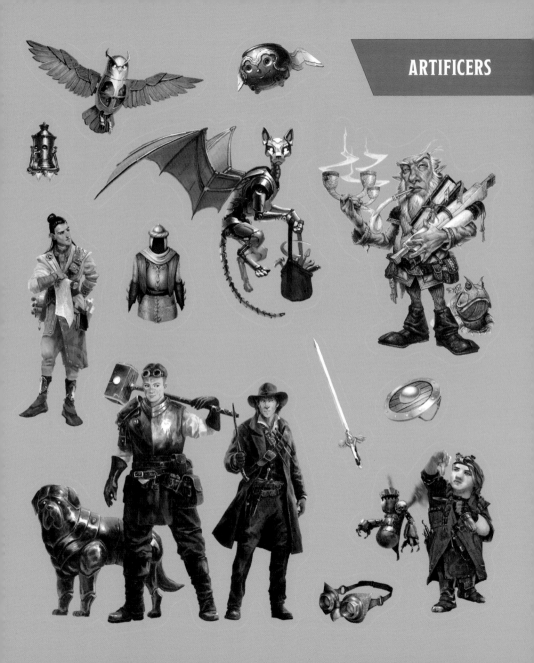

ARTIFICERS

Masters of invention, artificers use ingenuity and magic to unlock extraordinary capabilities in objects. Few characters can produce the right tool for a job as well as these can.

HOMUNCULUS SERVANTS

EFREETI CHAIN MAIL

ROCK GNOME ARTIFICER

SHIELD

DANCING SWORD

HUMAN ARTIFICERS

GNOME ARTIFICER

GOGGLES OF NIGHT

MAGIC, WEAPONS & TREASURE

TALISMAN OF ULTIMATE EVIL

ORB OF DRAGONKIND

The proper gear can mean the difference between life or death for an adventurer. If you're lucky or courageous, you might uncover a magical item or two that will help bolster your victory against a villain.

SATCHEL

MANTLE OF MAGIC RESISTANCE

TALISMAN OF THE SPHERE

MEDALLION OF THOUGHTS

AXE OF MIGHTY CLEAVING

ARROW OF DRAGON SLAYING

ROD OF CANCELLATION

ROD OF RULERSHIP

STAFF OF ILLUSION

MACE OF DISRUPTION

COINS OF THE REALMS

MAGIC, WEAPONS & TREASURE

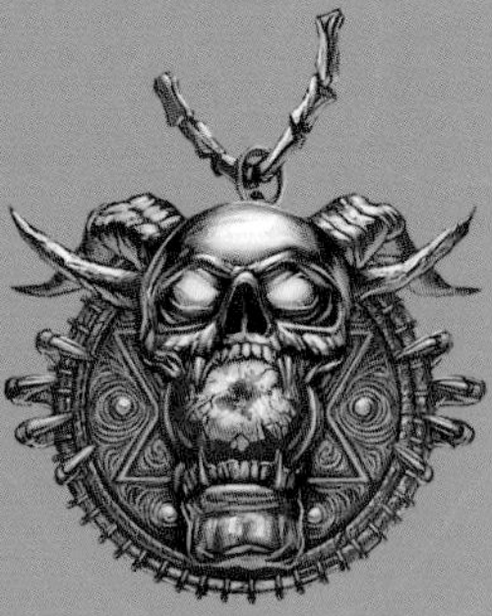
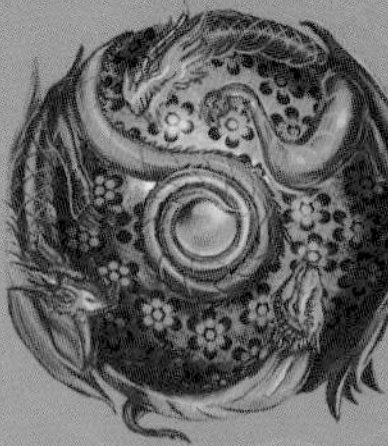
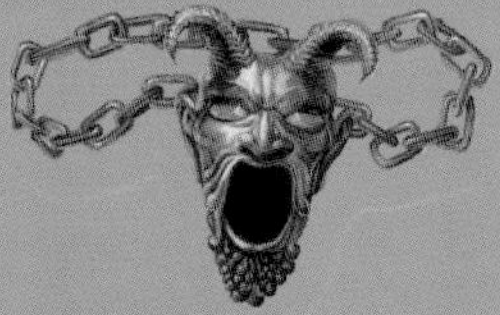
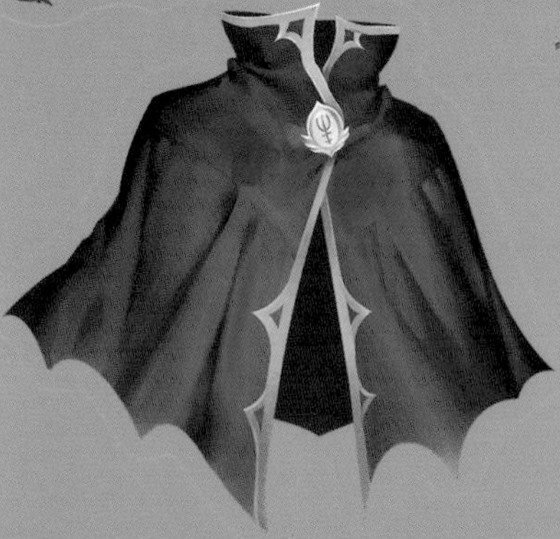
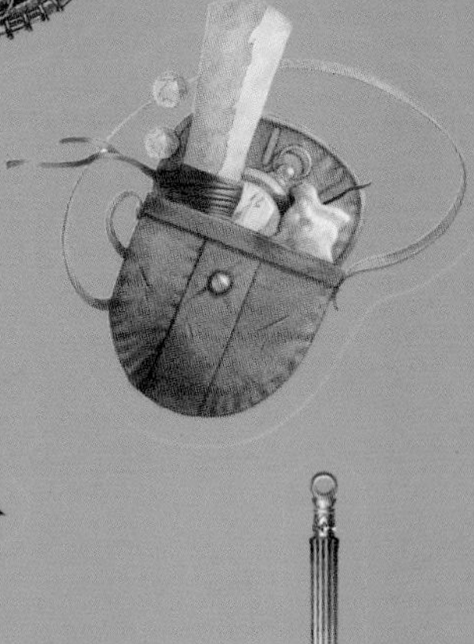
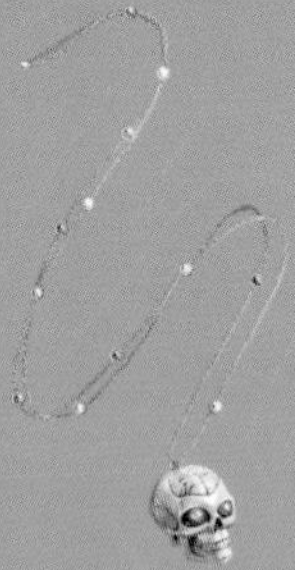
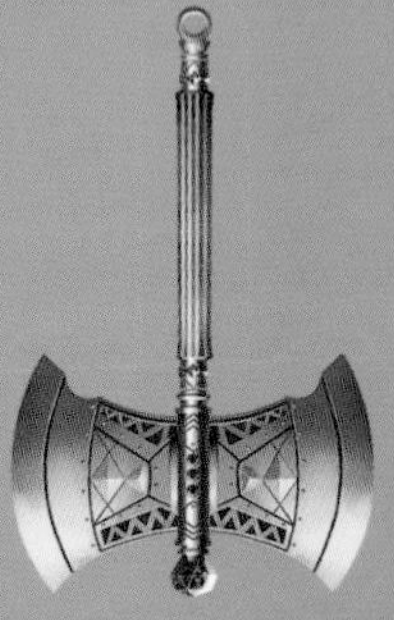
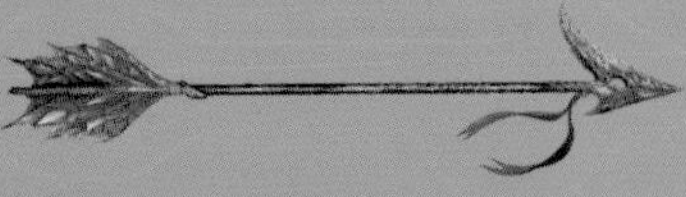
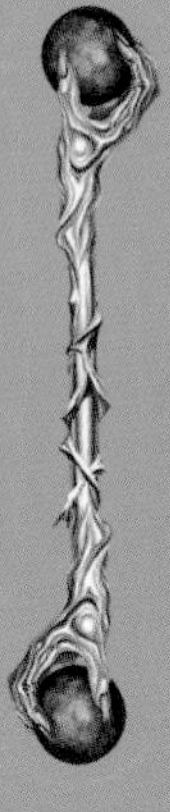
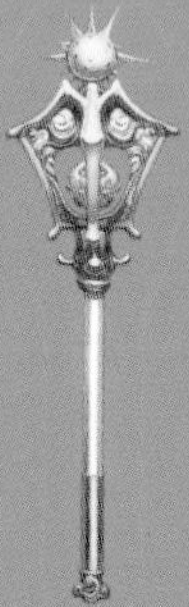
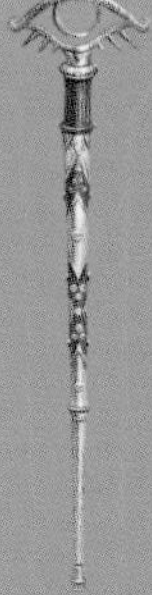
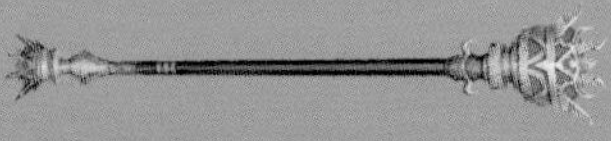
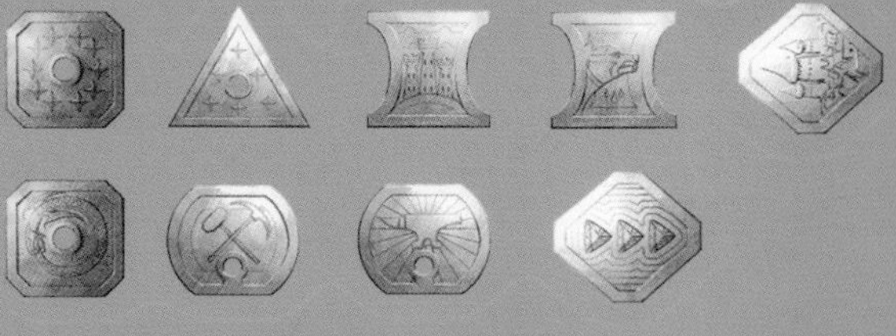

CUBIC GATE

DAGGER OF VENOM

HELMET OF TELEPATHY

HORN OF VALHALLA

RING OF EVASION

FROST BRAND

FLAME TONGUE

BOOTS OF SPEED

WINGED BOOTS

HAMMER OF THUNDERBOLTS

BOOK OF EXALTED DEEDS

GAUNTLETS OF OGRE POWER

GIANT SLAYER

KENKU

Cursed and stripped of their wings, these birdlike humanoids have a secretive nature and typically work as spies or thieves but can be good allies.

Heroes come in many shapes and sizes. These four characters were introduced in *Volo's Guide to Monsters* and *Mordenkainen Presents: Monsters of the Multiverse* and have since become fan favorites.

TABAXI

Created by the Cat Lord—a divine being of the Upper Planes—to blend the qualities of humanoids and cats, tabaxi are a varied people in both attitude and appearance. In some lands, they live like cats, naturally curious and at home in playful environments. In other places, they live as other folk do, not exhibiting the feline behavior the Cat Lord intended.

TORTLE

Humanoid tortoises are a peaceful and patient species that are born on the sandy coasts but grow up to lead lives of adventure as nomadic survivalists.

HARENGON

These rabbitfolk originated in the Feywild, where they spoke Sylvan and embodied the spirit of freedom and travel. In time, harengon hopped into other worlds, bringing the fey realm's dangers during adventures.

SUN

KEY

SKULL

KNIGHT

JESTER

DONJON

DECK OF MANY THINGS

Usually found in a box or pouch, this deck contains a number of cards (either 13 or 22 cards) made of ivory or vellum. You must declare how many cards you intend to draw from the deck and then draw them randomly. As soon as you draw a card from the deck, its magic takes effect.

The Dwarvish language of Faerûn uses a runic alphabet called Dethk. You can find ancient inscriptions carved onto weapons, stone buildings, or magic items. Use this runic script to craft your own message or help decipher one.

A	B	C	D	E	F	G	H	I	J	K	L	M

N	O	P	Q	R	S	T	U	V	W	X	Y	Z

DWARVISH SCRIPT

A	B	C	D	E	F	G	H	I	J	K	L	M
<	T	]	٩	₹	Ⲣ	ꓵ	+	⺈	Ⴈ	⋗	Ⳑ	ⱳ
<	T	]	٩	₹	Ⲣ	ꓵ	+	⺈	Ⴈ	⋗	Ⳑ	ⱳ
<	T	]	٩	₹	Ⲣ	ꓵ	+	⺈	Ⴈ	⋗	Ⳑ	ⱳ
<	T	]	٩	₹	Ⲣ	ꓵ	+	⺈	Ⴈ	⋗	Ⳑ	ⱳ
<	T	]	٩	₹	Ⲣ	ꓵ	+	⺈	Ⴈ	⋗	Ⳑ	ⱳ
<	T	]	٩	₹	Ⲣ	ꓵ	+	⺈	Ⴈ	⋗	Ⳑ	ⱳ

N	O	P	Q	R	S	T	U	V	W	X	Y	Z
₹	∩	Γ	I	Ⴀ	⟩	Ⲣ	↲	ꓷ	⺌	⟩	Π	₹
₹	∩	Γ	I	Ⴀ	⟩	Ⲣ	↲	ꓷ	⺌	⟩	Π	₹
₹	∩	Γ	I	Ⴀ	⟩	Ⲣ	↲	ꓷ	⺌	⟩	Π	₹
₹	∩	Γ	I	Ⴀ	⟩	Ⲣ	↲	ꓷ	⺌	⟩	Π	₹
₹	∩	Γ	I	Ⴀ	⟩	Ⲣ	↲	ꓷ	⺌	⟩	Π	₹
₹	∩	Γ	I	Ⴀ	⟩	Ⲣ	↲	ꓷ	⺌	⟩	Π	₹

A	B	C	D	E	F	G	H	I	J	K	L	M
ȸ	ȸ	ȸ	ȸ	ȸ	ȸ	ȸ	ȸ	ȸ	ȸ	ȸ	ȸ	ȸ
ȸ	ȸ	ȸ	ȸ	ȸ	ȸ	ȸ	ȸ	ȸ	ȸ	ȸ	ȸ	ȸ
ȸ	ȸ	ȸ	ȸ	ȸ	ȸ	ȸ	ȸ	ȸ	ȸ	ȸ	ȸ	ȸ
ȸ	ȸ	ȸ	ȸ	ȸ	ȸ	ȸ	ȸ	ȸ	ȸ	ȸ	ȸ	ȸ
ȸ	ȸ	ȸ	ȸ	ȸ	ȸ	ȸ	ȸ	ȸ	ȸ	ȸ	ȸ	ȸ
ȸ	ȸ	ȸ	ȸ	ȸ	ȸ	ȸ	ȸ	ȸ	ȸ	ȸ	ȸ	ȸ

N	O	P	Q	R	S	T	U	V	W	X	Y	Z
ȸ	ȸ	ȸ	ȸ	ȸ	ȸ	ȸ	ȸ	ȸ	ȸ	ȸ	ȸ	ȸ
ȸ	ȸ	ȸ	ȸ	ȸ	ȸ	ȸ	ȸ	ȸ	ȸ	ȸ	ȸ	ȸ
ȸ	ȸ	ȸ	ȸ	ȸ	ȸ	ȸ	ȸ	ȸ	ȸ	ȸ	ȸ	ȸ
ȸ	ȸ	ȸ	ȸ	ȸ	ȸ	ȸ	ȸ	ȸ	ȸ	ȸ	ȸ	ȸ
ȸ	ȸ	ȸ	ȸ	ȸ	ȸ	ȸ	ȸ	ȸ	ȸ	ȸ	ȸ	ȸ
ȸ	ȸ	ȸ	ȸ	ȸ	ȸ	ȸ	ȸ	ȸ	ȸ	ȸ	ȸ	ȸ

ELVISH SCRIPT

The language of Elves is fluid with subtle intonations and intricate grammar. Elven literature is rich and varied, and their songs and poems are famous among other species. Many bards learn their language so they can play Elvish ballads. Use this alphabet to write your own poetry or lyrics.

The ancient language of the dragons, Draconic is thought to be one of the oldest languages and is often used in the study of magic. The language sounds harsh to most other creatures and includes numerous hard consonants and sibilants. Use these runic characters to communicate with a dragon or decipher a message.

A	B	C	D	E	F	G	H	I	J	K	L	M

N	O	P	Q	R	S	T	U	V	W	X	Y	Z

DRACONIC SCRIPT

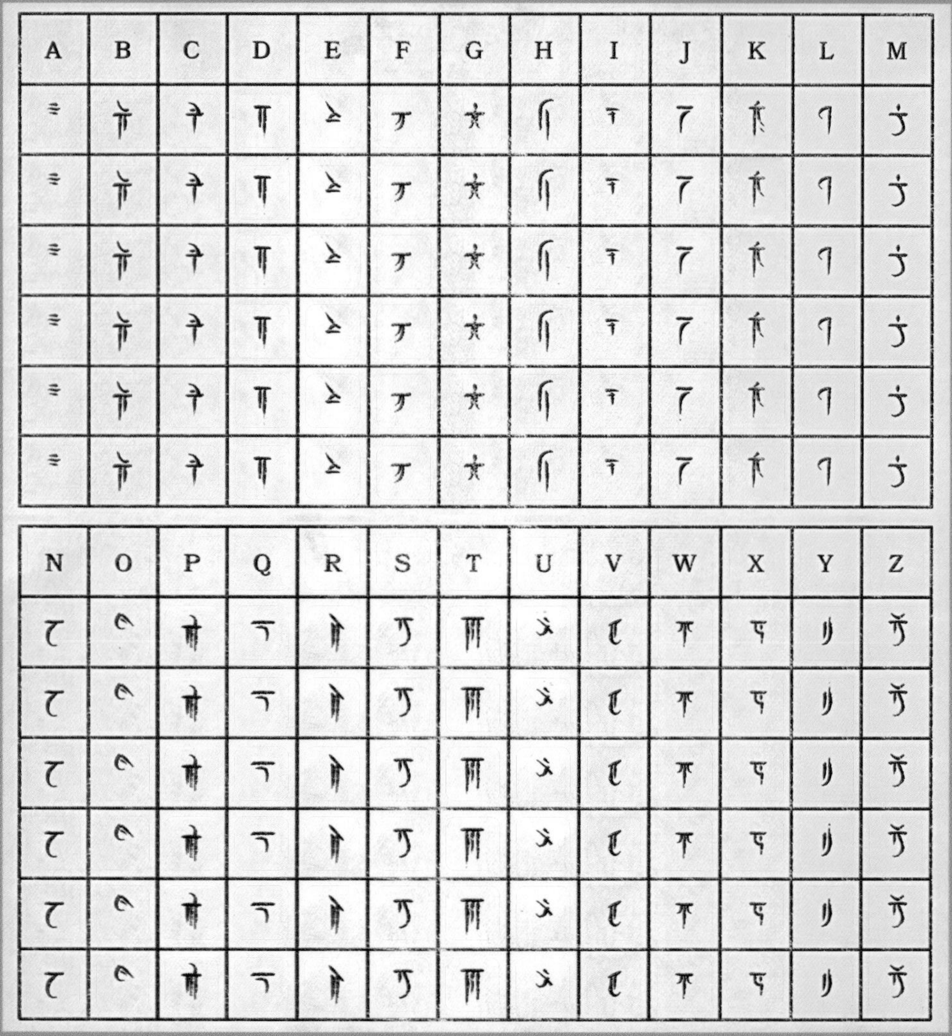
A B C D E F G H I J K L M
N O P Q R S T U V W X Y Z